Momilies®
As My Mother
Used to Say...®

Momilies®
As My Mother Used to Say...®

Michele Slung

BALLANTINE BOOKS • NEW YORK

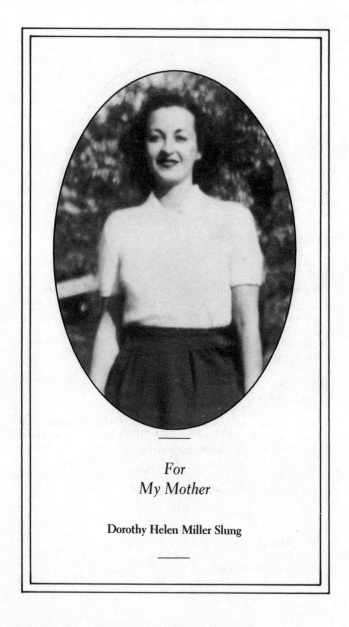

For
My Mother

Dorothy Helen Miller Slung

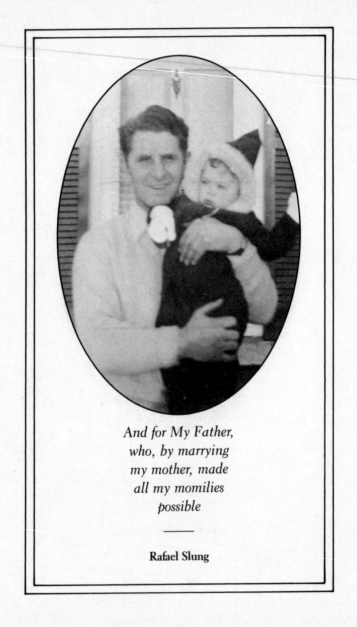

*And for My Father,
who, by marrying
my mother, made
all my momilies
possible*

———

Rafael Slung

CONTENTS

Introduction to the Anniversary Edition

In the early spring of 1985, I found myself doing something rather thrilling that, until then, I'd only seen people do in the movies: boarding a plane with no luggage to speak of, using a ticket purchased at the airline counter mere minutes earlier. What's more, my parents, whom I was on my way to see, hadn't the slightest idea I was about to show up.

My destination was Pompano Beach, Florida; my mother and father had retired there a decade earlier from Kentucky, where I'd grown up. I was—and am—an only child, and my arriving unannounced was entirely unusual. Unexpected visits were not part of the Slung family repertoire, and, to raise the excitement stakes, this was a surprise that actually had another, even more unexpected surprise contained within it.

Nervously, I kept checking to see that the small paperback book, which was the reason for my impromptu journey, was safely tucked in my bag. In truth, I was probably taking it out over and over for my own pleasure, as much to convince myself that it really existed as for reassurance that my sole copy hadn't suddenly vanished.

Ever since I'd begun working on *Momilies*® *As My Mother Used To Say . . .*®—inspired by my mother and paying amused, affectionate homage to the power of moms everywhere—I'd vowed that the moment I had the first book off the press I'd hop in a cab to the airport. I'd kept the project a secret for the entire year I'd been compiling it, and presenting my mother with her copy as a bolt from the publishing blue, just like this, had always been the plan.

It was an opportunity I knew would not come again, a chance to hand her something that not only paid public tribute to her enduring influence on me but also featured a gorgeous picture of her—looking just as I remembered her when I was a little girl—for all the world to see.

When I rang the bell to their apartment, my parents were dumbfounded, to say the least. "Michele? Michele Slung?" my mother demanded over the intercom, certain I must be a trickster pretending to be her distant daughter. Yet within a few minutes I was upstairs at her door, thrusting the book into her hands as she stepped back to let me in.

Barely glancing at it, she was intent, as usual, on examining me and trying to figure out whether my appearance gave some clue as to why I was there. "Look at it!" I urged her. She did her best to comply, but my standing in front of her, in the flesh with no warning, continued to be too much for her to take in. No precedents existed.

"Sit down! Come on, sit down! Please!" Still in shock, she remained on her feet, reluctant. At this point, my father, now curious himself, joined in. "Come on, Dorothy, sit down. Michele's not going anywhere."

So my mother nervously perched on the edge of a

kitchen chair, opened *Momilies* and slowly began to read. (She skipped the book's opening pages, thus missing her photo, and I had to point it out later.) We both watched her. No one said anything. Soon a smile crossed her face, then she started to chuckle. She looked up at me for a second. I grinned.

"What do you think?

She shook her head. "In a minute," she said. "I want to finish it." My father and I watched and waited.

"So," I said, starting to get impatient. "Have you recognized your own 'Momilies'? It's a test."

I was only half teasing.

"Just a second." She flipped back through the pages.

"Okay. Here are some." She paused, then began to list them: "You're not the only pebble on the beach. Wish on your eyelash and blow it away. I don't care whether you like them or not—you're related. I'm only doing this for your own good. The more you scratch it the more it's going to itch. Lift up your legs when you go over a railroad track and make a wish. Wash behind your ears or you'll have a potato field growing back there."

She took a breath, then continued, "Always clean up in the kitchen as you go along. Don't raise your eyes to heaven, God won't help you. How can you tell what it looks like if you don't try it on? Put some color in your cheeks. Throw your shoulders back and you won't feel so cold. Always put the zipper on the inside of the pillow case so you won't cut your face at night.

Don't go out of the house with wet hair or you'll get a cold."

I marveled. "That's amazing. I didn't think you would have remembered that you said all those things."

"I didn't," my mother replied. She had a funny expression on her face. "I didn't know I said them at all. The ones I just repeated were the ones my mother said to me. I could hear her voice as I went through the book, whenever I saw one of hers I remembered."

And because her mother had died when she was fifteen, I'd never known my maternal grandmother. My mother began to cry. In every way, it was too much for her.

That was March of 1985. By May and Mother's Day, I was exhilarated by my travels across the country talking about *Momilies.* It had made all the national bestseller lists, and Ballantine Books, the publisher, was already asking for a sequel for the following year. My mother was a minor local celebrity— at least in her condo complex—and my father was starting to let his jealousy show.

By the time *More Momilies* was published in 1986, which I cleverly dedicated it to my dad ("who, by marrying my mother, made all my 'Momilies' possible"), my mother had taken to carrying her copy in her purse at all times, wrapped snugly in a protective plastic bag. After all, you never could tell when there might be someone new to show it to. Being the

"Mom" of *Momilies* was an exciting, thoroughly enjoyable role for her and not one she took lightly.

Now it's the 20th anniversary of the publication of both books. They have remained in print, have been released as an audio book, and have also been translated into other languages, including German, Italian, French, and Japanese. Over the past two decades I've had hundreds of letters from people wanting to share their own "Momilies" and family anecdotes with me, and I've talked to probably hundreds and hundreds more on radio phone-in shows, many of whom seemed to think it was their mom and their mom alone who signaled caution when it came to strange toilet seats. In 1996, the two books were combined into a single volume.

It's hard for me to remember a time before *Momilies*—and I know my mother doesn't.

Just as I intended, it was the best present I ever gave her.

Author's Notes

Nothing seems to lodge in the mind so securely as the well-turned maternal phrase. Listen to your conversations and notice how frequently you offer up a maxim or a piece of advice that begins, "As my mother used to say . . ." Most children grow up and realize, at some rather wrenching moment, that Mom is fallible, maybe not even the smartest woman in the world, but by then it's too late—what she's said is what you've got.

Momilies® get repeated from generation to generation, and sometimes the original meaning is lost, yet the sense remains. Many of them are all-purpose, a few are cruel, the majority loving; what's amazing is how, year in, year out, they guide our behavior, in ways both large and small. Momilies have no real geographic or class lines; they transcend most human divisions. All you need to do is think of one of your mother's favorite sayings and her voice is magically in your ear.

Whether you like it or not.

—May 1985

The idea for the book that became *Momilies: As My Mother Used to Say* had its origins in my passion for making lists. Thinking one day of that particular phrase which my own mother had produced on so many occasions (when I seemed to be taking an overinflated view of myself)—"You're not the only pebble on the beach" was what she'd say, ominously—led me to wonder how many other of her familiar utterances I could call to mind.

Not so surprisingly, it wasn't difficult to come up with more, once I cast my ear back to my childhood: "Always clean up in the kitchen as you go along." "You can't tell what it looks like until you try it on." "You don't have to *like* them; they're your relatives." "Put some color in your cheeks." "The more you scratch it, the more it's going to itch."

The list grew longer and longer. And once I started with my own, I began to be curious whether everyone else possessed equally unforgettable maternal maxims. So I started asking friends and the friends of friends. To my delight, practically all of them quickly emerged as zealous "momily" recollectors! Postcards came in the mail; there were momily messages on my answering machine. And I became a connoisseur of the especially eccentric or useful ones.

When someone turned out to be a bit uncertain just what a "momily" was, I'd say simply, "It's anything your mother told you that you've never forgotten." No matter what kind of wisdom or wackiness the momily contains, my definition of it also holds that if it still zings into your mind on the proper occasion, if you can still hear your mom's tender (or sarcastic, or hectoring) voice, then what you've got is the genuine article.

More Momilies: As My Mother Used to Say, is the result of new friends and readers—people across North America, from Shreveport to Saskatchewan, even across the Pacific, from Hartford to Honolulu—enthusiastically sharing their "momilies" with me. Having put a name to the phenomenon (phe-*mom*-enon?), I heard from men and women both old and young, from the children of Irish, Italian, Swedish, Dutch, Greek, French, Hungarian—you name the nationality or religion!—mothers. It didn't take long for me to see just how "momilies" were a sort of universal language.

Naturally, I'd suspected this must be so—after all, how many times was I told "Everyone has a mom?"—but it was truly wonderful, even downright exciting, to have it proved so conclusively, over and over again.

—May 1986

Momilies®
As My Mother
Used to Say...®

Anna Hall Roosevelt

Mother Knows Best

I'm only doing this for your own good.

———

It's only your mother who's going to tell you the truth.

———

You only nag the ones you love.

———

As long as I'm around, I'll be your mother.

———

When my eyes close, yours will open.

3

Rebecca Rushall Friedman

You can be sure of two things in this world: there is a God, and your mother loves you.

———

If somebody else's mother lets him jump off the Empire State Building, would you want me to let you do it, too?

———

Don't worry, there are plenty of fish in the sea.

———

A little of what you fancy does you good.

———

You can't be in twelve places with one behind.

———

You can't put one foot in two shoes at the same time.

———

You pays your money and you takes your choice.

———

If the French were so intelligent, they'd speak English.

———

In matters of taste, there is no disputing.

———

If your manners are perfect on the surface, you can be as unconventional as you wish, underneath.

———

When in doubt, write a thank-you note.

Minna Schoenberg Marx

A bored person is a boring person.

———

All a little girl has to do is be amiable.

———

A playboy's nothing but a high-class bum.

———

A doctor's never the richest man in town, but he's always well-respected.

———

They've got orange peels on the slop pile—they must be rich.

———

Some folks make a dollar a day and spend a dollar and a dime.

———

The best sleep is the sleep you get before midnight.

———

Nothing worthwhile happens after midnight.

———

You have to get up in the middle of the night to fool your mother.

Amelia Keyser Stein

"Just You Wait..."

Be careful what you wish for; you might get it.

———

Someday you boys are going to have to serve your country.

———

Whistling girls and crowing hens always come to some bad end.

———

If I had talked to your grandmother the way you talk to me . . .

Amalie Nathanson Freud

I suppose you think you're not going to be a parent one day too.

Louisa Van Velsor Whitman

"I Mean Business"

I don't care if Jesus Christ himself is tap dancing on TV, turn if off and come to dinner this minute.

———

As long as you live under my roof, you'll do as I say.

———

I'm not asking you—I'm telling you.

———

That's not a request—it's an order.

———

Don't ask me *why*. The answer is *no*.

13

Lydia Beardsall Lawrence

You don't have to like me, buster—I'm your mother.

———

This is not a hotel.

———

Don't treat me like a kid—I'm your mother.

———

And don't come into my bedroom unless you're bleeding.

Charlotte Stearns Eliot

"Go Ahead–Be Bad"

You must think rules are made to be broken.

———

If you're quiet, you must be up to no good.

———

You'll learn—pigs always get into trouble.

———

Doing bad was never in God's plan—if you blame Him, you're a fool.

17

Anna Mathilda McNeill Whistler

Your ducks will come home to roost.

———

You have to have an answer for everything, don't you?

Agnes Louise Crookenden Olivier

Putting You In Your Place

Just because parents are allowed to do something doesn't mean kids get to do the same thing.

———

Everybody else may be doing it, but you're not going to.

———

Oh, so it's the egg teaching the chicken!

———

If you can't say anything nice, don't say anything at all.

———

He who toots his own horn never gets tooted.

21

Grace Hall Hemingway

Bragging doesn't become you.

———

You're not the only pebble on the beach.

———

The sun doesn't rise and set around you.

———

Did you meet anyone today you liked better than yourself?

———

You won't be happy until you're crying.

———

So it's raining? You're not sugar—you won't melt.

———

You can dish it out, but you can't take it.

———

When your head swells ups, your brain stops working.

———

Be a big wheel if you want—just remember that little dogs go to the bathroom on big wheels.

———

The bigger you get, the more stupid you are.

———

Nobody likes a funny kid.

Lela Owens McMath

You'll never be hung for your beauty.

Fools' names, like fools' faces, are always seen in public places.

_____

Only two kinds of people complain of the cold: paupers and fools.

_____

Don't be so scared—if it doesn't have teeth, it won't bite you.

_____

Little animals don't eat big ones.

_____

Are you a man or a mouse?

_____

There's room for everyone at the table—except the Devil.

_____

You've buttered your bed—now lie on it.

_____

Why do you think I have gray hairs?

Sara Warmbrodt Taylor

The World Is A Dangerous Place

Remember the three B's: be careful, be good, and be home early.

———

Whenever you leave the house, put a dime in your shoe—in case you have to make a phone call.

———

Always give a penny to a poor old man—he may be Jesus in disguise testing you.

———

Never trust a man who wears a metal watchband.

———

I'd trust that man as far as I could sling a piano.

Anna Johnson LeSueur

Never be in bed during a thunderstorm.

———

Never use the plumbing during a thunderstorm.

———

Sit in the middle of the living room during a thunderstorm.

———

Never drink out of a water fountain—you don't know who's been there before you.

———

Always put toilet paper on the seat.

———

Put that down! You don't know where it's been!

———

A dog always knows when you're afraid of it.

———

Don't take rides from strangers.

———

Don't take candy from strangers.

———

Don't go into dark alleys.

———

. . . And don't go near any cliffs.

Hulda Minthorn Hoover

"You'll Regret It"

Don't cross your eyes or they'll freeze that way.

If you swallow the stone, a cherry tree grows in your stomach.

If you swallow your gum, a horse will grow in your stomach.

Never nap after a meal or you'll get fat.

Don't put anything wet on the bed.

31

Mildred Frances Cowan Turner

Don't lean back in the movies or you'll get ringworm.

———

Don't run with a lollipop in your mouth.

———

If you go to bed with wet hair, you'll be gray before you're thirty.

———

Don't wear good underwear to the doctor or your bill will be higher.

———

Never learn how to iron a man's shirt or you'll wind up having to do it.

———

Don't sit too close to the television, it'll ruin your eyes.

———

Never try on anyone else's glasses or you'll go blind.

———

If you don't wash your hands after you go to the bathroom, it'll go to your brain.

———

Don't hit your mother or your hand will come out of your grave.

Rosalie Mercurio DiMaggio

Some Don'ts

Don't do anything you wouldn't do if I were sitting on your shoulder.

―――

Don't start anything you don't plan to finish.

―――

Don't let your emotions rule your head.

―――

Don't say no without thinking twice.

―――

Don't expect too much and you'll never be disappointed.

Henrietta Trisch Willkie

Don't expect from people what they're not capable of giving.

———

Don't bother to get angry at people who don't matter to you.

———

Don't let grass grow under your pencil—go ahead and do your homework.

———

Don't be a Philadelphia lawyer.

———

Don't say "drapes."

———

Don't sleep with the bedspread on the bed.

———

Don't put any beans up your nose.

Odessa Grady Clay

Running
Away

Is that a threat or a promise?

—

If you leave, don't come back.

—

If you leave, it's easy to show me your back, but when you come back you have to show me your face.

—

Good, I'll pack your lunch.

Aloise Steiner Buckley

Mom Tries Sarcasm

Excuse me for living.

———

Don't say "she"! Who's "she"? The *cat's* mother?

———

Why don't you go out and play on the yellow line?

———

I can't shoot you—there's a law against it.

———

If you get separated from me in the crowd . . . write.

———

If your ship doesn't come in, maybe your canoe will.   41

Nancy Elliott Edison

"You Can Do It!"

If a thing is worth doing, it's worth doing well.

———

Everybody has to do the best with what he's got.

———

Everybody makes his own contribution.

———

Never say "never."

———

Show 'em greatness.

Josephine Lee Price

He's no better than you—we all stand up naked inside our clothes.

———

You're not in competition with anyone but yourself.

———

Anyone's a fool who doesn't try to live up to his dreams and abilities.

———

Every time you give up pleasure for duty, you're a stronger person.

———

Keep all strings a' drawing.

———

Don't dawdle—quick's the word and sharp's the action!

Paula Stern Kissinger

Ladies And Gentlemen

A lady always has a clean handkerchief, gloves, and a hat.

———

A lady always has a handkerchief and pocket money.

———

A lady never uses a toothpick.

———

A lady never smokes on the street.

———

A lady doesn't swear aloud.

Jeanne Weil Proust

A skirt should be tight enough to show you're a woman, but loose enough to show you're a lady.

———

A lady never sits with her knees parted.

———

Horses sweat, men perspire, ladies glow.

———

Every house has to have at least one lady.

———

Call her a woman . . . we don't know if she's a lady.

———

"Gentlemen" is a word that gentlemen never use, but ladies sometimes have to.

———

A gentleman doesn't strike a lady.

———

Nice people don't put cream in their after-dinner coffee.

———

No one in our family would drink beer out of a can.

Susan Tadd Graham

What You Wear

Always put on clean underwear in the morning, in case you're in an accident.

———

Go ahead and try it on—you can't compare yourself to a hanger.

———

Who's paying for all these clothes, anyway?

———

I didn't buy all these clothes just to decorate your closet.

———

Always buy one good dress instead of three cheap ones.   51

Jennie Jerome Churchill

The important thing is to get a good bra.

———

Are you sure there's enough room in the crotch?

———

An extra half-inch at the end of your hem is like an extra half-inch at the end of your nose.

———

Your shoes should always be darker than your hemline.

———

Always wear your strings of pearls in odd numbers.

———

Always wear a coat and tie when you go on an airplane.

———

White is not a winter color.

———

Don't wear white until Easter or after Labor Day.

———

Blue and green should never be seen.

———

Brown is a neutral color.

———

Don't take off your sweaters before May.

———

Save your lace for your nighties.

Georgie Drew Barrymore

Lovers shouldn't wear linen.

———

It's not what you wear; it's who you are.

Nellie Ruth Pillsbury King

The Way
You Look

If you want to be beautiful, you have to be willing to suffer a little.

———

You've got a face only a mother could love.

———

You'll never be a picture.

———

Pretty doesn't hurt.

———

If you carry yourself like a beauty, people will think of you as one.

Sarah Morse Borden

First thing when you wake up in the morning, go to the mirror and smile.

———

Get your hair out of your eyes.

———

Put some color in your cheeks.

———

Take off some of that lipstick—your mouth looks like a chicken's ass in pokeberry time.

———

Tan fat looks better than pale fat.

———

Don't worry—it's only baby fat.

———

Sit up straight.

———

Throw your shoulders back and you won't feel so cold.

———

Stick out your chest—here comes the iceman.

———

Clean your glasses—you can't be optimistic with a misty optic.

———

Wash behind your ears or you'll have a potato field growing back there.

Polly Scobell Cartland

It's no disgrace to get head lice, but it is to keep them.

_____

The only thing that counts in a job interview is clean fingernails.

_____

Wash your elbows whenever you have the opportunity.

_____

Put on hand lotion every time you think of it.

_____

For every white hair you pluck out, two more will grow in.

_____

Girls who pierce their ears are no better than they should be.

_____

Nice girls don't wear ankle bracelets.

_____

Only sluts wear half-slips.

Cynthia Stanton Baum

Around
The House

How come you always offer to do the dishes at other people's houses?

———

Here's how you help: first, you take the dishes off the table.

———

It's just as easy to wash a dish well as it is to wash it badly.

———

Always clean up in the kitchen as you go along.

Gertrude Creiger Temple

Close the door behind you—were you born in a jail?

———

Never answer the phone on the first ring.

———

I know if you clean up your room, it's bound to rain.

———

I don't see any hooks on that floor.

———

A drop of oil or a drop of spit works wonders.

———

Leave a dead fly and others gather.

———

Always put the zipper on the inside of a pillow case so you won't cut your face at night.

———

Sleep tight and don't let the bedbugs bite.

———

Wake up, snakes, and crawl! June bugs are hopping!

———

You have to make your bed in case the house burns.

———

How can you sleep in an unmade bed?

Helen Lena Fritsche Cronkite

Foodstuff

Think of all the starving children in China (India, Armenia, etc.).

———

If you don't clean your plate, you won't get any dessert.

———

If you eat all your carrots, you'll be able to see in the dark.

———

Eat your fish—it's brain food.

———

All the vitamins are in the skin.

67

Adèle-Eugénie-Sidonie Landoy Colette

The crust is the best part of the bread.

―――

Eat the crusts of your bread so your hair will get nice and curly.

―――

When a date takes you out for dinner, never order chicken or spaghetti because there's no way to eat either neatly.

―――

Why do you want to order that out, when you can get it at home?

―――

Don't eat chocolate ice cream—it's made of left-over vanilla.

―――

Crabs and ice cream don't mix.

―――

I scream, you scream, we all scream for ice cream.

―――

Don't eat milk with tuna fish—you'll get hives.

―――

If you eat too many doughnuts, you'll turn into one.

―――

If you don't eat your okra, you won't catch any fish.

Margaret Majer Kelly

You can't start the day on an empty stomach.

———

You can't read and digest at the same time.

———

Thirty-seven chews to a bite!

———

Chew your bananas.

———

Drink tea only out of a china teacup.

———

A good housewife always has lemons in her refrigerator.

———

It's a sin to put even bread crumbs on the fire.

———

If there's enough, put a crust on it; if there isn't, make it into soup.

———

The better the butter, the better the batter.

———

Cold food gives you a bellyache.

———

Don't turn up your nose!

———

It all winds up in the same place anyway.

71

Ella Quinlan O'Neill

"Let Me Feel Your Forehead"

If it didn't taste bad, it wouldn't be medicine.

———

Don't go in the water for an hour after eating.

———

Don't go out of the house with your hair wet or you'll get a cold.

———

Sneakers ruin your feet.

———

The more you scratch it, the more it's going to itch.

73

Abigail May Alcott

It'll never get well if you pick it.

———

Don't stifle a sneeze.

———

Don't get someone else's breath, and you'll never get sick.

———

If any germ survives that, it's your friend.

———

The night air will make you sick.

———

Eat local honey—wherever you go—to avoid allergies.

———

If you have a head, you have headaches.

Pauline Koch Einstein

Love
And
Marriage

It's just as easy to fall in love with a rich man as a poor one.

———

Don't marry for money—marry where money is.

———

She who marries for money, earns it.

———

Throw yourself at a man's head and you'll land at his feet.

———

You don't have to marry every boy you go out with.

Ethel Milne Gumm

You don't want to chase a man and get him, because then he'll always remember how he was gotten.

———

Anyone who'd run away with you would drop you at the first lamppost.

———

If he tries to kiss you, call me.

———

Don't be such a smarty-pants—you'll scare the boys away.

———

You'll never get a boyfriend if you don't learn to play bridge.

———

Girls are like streetcars—there'll be another one along in ten minutes.

———

When you're on a date, order one drink and sip it slowly.

———

If you marry a gentile, he'll beat you and drink.

———

Don't marry anyone until you've seen them drunk.

———

A man without a good appetite for food won't have a good appetite for anything else.

Frances Zuchowski Liberace

Save yourself for your husband.

———

Why should a farmer buy a cow when he can get the milk for free?

———

I knew he wasn't right for you, anyway.

———

What does his father do?

Mary America Rogers

Relatively Speaking

No matter what happens, you'll always have your family.

———

You can choose your friends, but you can't choose your relatives.

———

I don't care whether you like them or not—you're related.

———

Treat your friends like family and your family like friends.

Margaret Isabella Balfour Stevenson

Wait 'til your brother cries for an hour before you give in.

———

If you can't get along with your brothers and sisters, how can you expect to get along with the world?

———

Elsie Kingdome Leach

A Few Superstitions

Wish on your eyelash and blow it away.

———

Lift up your legs when you go over a railroad track and make a wish.

———

Always eat the tip of a piece of pie last and make a wish on it.

———

Never start a trip on a Friday.

Julie Löwy Kafka

Never kill a spider—it'll bring bad luck.

———

Don't ever talk about the future and forget to say "God willing."

Cleo Sisco Gurley

Proverbial Wisdom

Two wrongs don't make a right.

———

The apple doesn't fall far from the tree.

———

Water seeks its own level.

———

A miss is as good as a mile.

———

Imitation is the sincerest form of flattery.

Sarah Glantz Berlinger

A fool and his money are soon parted.

———

You can't judge a book by its cover.

———

In the dark all cats are gray.

———

The way to a man's heart is through his stomach.

———

It's no use crying over spilt milk; there's enough water in it already.

———

Handsome is as handsome does.

———

You can't make a silk purse out of a sow's ear.

———

You catch more flies with honey than with vinegar.

———

Pride goes before a fall.

———

If wishes were horses, beggars would ride.

———

If my grandmother had wheels, she'd be an omnibus.

Lucy Read Anthony

The Dress Question

Put on your sweater—I'm cold.

Are you sure you're warm enough?

Always wear a white collar. It brightens your face.

Never wear red, or you'll be taken for a hussy.

Earrings that dangle are not for daytime.

Eliza Grace Symonds Bell

It doesn't matter what you wear on a Friday.

———

Wearing hats make you go bald.

———

Always take a bath before putting on clean underwear.

———

Gentlemen are known by their heels.

———

Don't ever go outside wearing slippers.

———

No matter how poor you are, wear expensive shoes.

———

It's . . . okay. But you can find something nicer.

———

Cheap is cheap.

Irena Spenser Pym

"If I've Told You Once..."

Don't get smart with me.

———

Don't be a pill.

———

That's not a face I'd advise you to make too often.

———

Don't raise your eyes to heaven. God won't help you.

———

I'm not talking to you for my health.

Bernice Layne Brown

Look at me when I'm talking to you.

———

What I say goes in one ear and out the other.

———

Don't mumble. I graduated from mumbling school.

———

Didn't you know I've got eyes in the back of my head?

———

Do I look like a short-order cook?

———

I've only got one pair of hands.

———

You kids can fight. But you can't bite and scratch.

———

No matter *what* you're playing with, you can poke your eye out with it.

———

Don't ever put anything in your ear except your elbow.

———

Close your mouth before a fly gets in.

———

Don't bang the screen door!

———

Don't stand there dripping on the floor!

101

Mary Litogot Ford

Stick your head back in the window! Do you want to lose it?

———

You're going to break your neck!

———

If you fall out of that tree and break your leg, don't come running to me.

———

Why? Because "y" is a crooked letter.

———

Just because.

———

"Hey!" is for horses.

———

"Wait" broke the bridge.

———

Too much laughing leads to crying.

———

You children would try the patience of an iron saint.

Nell Carter Yule

What Are Mothers For?

Fool me once—
   Shame on you!
Fool me twice—
   Shame on me!

____

Do you think I got these bumps on my head from falling off a turnip?

____

I was your age once.

____

I could just eat you up.

105

Ida Stover Eisenhower

Every child in America is born to be president.

———

I'll forgive and I'll forget, but I'll remember.

———

I wouldn't give you a nickel for another one, but I wouldn't take a million for the ones I've got.

———

I've done my best. An angel could do no better.

———

Remember, I'm your mother—and you'll never have another.

———

Mothers know everything, except for things that change.

———

My mother didn't leave me anything of value except her wisdom.

———

Every day is children's day.

Lena Bogardus Phillips Lardner

Mom Sharpens Her Tongue

If I wanted to know your opinion, I'd ask for it.

———

I'm *not* everyone else's mom.

———

I've heard *that* one before.

———

Everything you're thinking about, I've already done.

———

Pretty is as pretty does, and you're pretty apt to stay that way.

109

Jane Lampton Clemens

You'd lose your head if it weren't tied on.

———

What did you do? Leave your brains at school?

———

If brains were dynamite, you wouldn't have enough to blow your nose.

———

You'd go to the ocean and not find any water.

———

Don't stand there grinning like a wave on a slop bucket.

———

So *who's* happy? Cows in the field are happy.

———

If you're born to hang, you won't drown.

———

Don't be stupid, stupid.

———

Try to pretend you're normal.

———

You call *that* a kiss?

Evangeline Lodge Land Lindbergh

Setting an Example

Why can't you be more like your brother [sister]?

———

It never hurts to be polite.

———

You can at least pretend to have a good time.

———

A lady doesn't keep people waiting.

———

Never ask personal questions.

Grace Caroline Swanson Hefner

Little children should be seen and not heard.

_____

Whistling's for loafers.

_____

Whistle before breakfast; cry before noon.

_____

An empty can makes the most noise; the same goes for heads.

_____

Don't talk with your mouth full.

_____

You only have so many words in your voice box.

_____

People spend too much time talking from their teeth out.

_____

The tongue, the tongue—we spend three years learning how to use it and the rest of our lives learning how to control it.

_____

If there's a silence, it's your fault.

_____

Share your toys.

_____

Good enough isn't good enough.

Lucetta Todhunter Stout

Good, better, best—
   Don't let it rest.
Until the good gets better,—
   And the better best.

———

God's work is done. Have you done *your* part?

———

Never do anything you wouldn't want to see published
in your hometown paper.

———

What will the neighbors think?

———

What would Jesus say?

Ann Geilus Austerlitz

Mom
Predicts

The day you're born is the day you draw your last peaceful breath.

———

You'll understand when you're older.

———

You'll get over it before you're married.

———

Wait until you grow a mustache.

———

Maybe in a year or two...

Molly McQuillan Fitzgerald

When they're little, they step on your toes.
When they're grown, they step on your heart.

———

You'll thank me someday.

———

You'll be sorry when I'm six feet under.

Amy Otis Earhart

Well, It Could Happen

Don't point—you'll get warts.

———

Don't sing at the table—you'll get a crazy wife.

———

Eat your beets so your cheeks will be pink.

———

Don't eat standing up—you'll get fat legs.

———

Burnt bread makes you pretty.

Ann Snyder Boothe

If you sew on a Sunday, you'll have to rip out all the stitches with your nose on Judgment Day.

———

Don't sit on the table, or you'll never get married.

———

If you wear hand-me-down shoes, you're stepping into someone else's problems.

———

Don't go around with one shoe on, or one of your parents will die.

———

Step on a crack; break your mother's back.

———

What falls on the floor arrives at the door:
a fork—a gawk
a knife—a wife
a spoon—a loon.

———

If your right palm itches, you're going to get money. If your left palm itches, you'll be in a fight.

Edwina Dakin Williams

Kiss your sister good night even if you're mad at her.
You don't know if you'll see her in the morning.

———

If you pout like that, a chicken's going to come and sit
on your lip.

Susan Phillips Lovecraft

"This Hurts Me More Than It Hurts You"

If you don't stop crying, I'll give you something to cry about.

————

If you don't stop that, I'm going to slap the black off of you.

————

If you don't watch out, I'll hang you by your toes.

————

I intend to spank you within an inch of your life.

129

Frances Allethea Murray Smith

If you can't behave, you're going to be eating off the mantelpiece.

———

Believe me, if you can't listen, you can feel.

———

That's just a taste of what you'll get next time.

———

Better you shed the tears than me.

———

I've killed kids for less than that.

———

If you don't think I mean it, just try me.

———

It's a lot hotter where you're going.

———

Wait till your father gets home.

Jean Harlow Carpenter

Take This to Heart

If it isn't yours, you don't want it.

——

When in doubt, say no.

——

Save your good times till later.

——

Don't we have enough trouble without borrowing it?

——

It's nice to be important but more important to be nice.   133

Gladys Smith Presley

Always tell the truth, even if you have to lie to do so.

———

I can forget and you can forget, but a piece of paper never forgets.

———

What you don't have in your head, you have to have in your heels.

———

When your mind doesn't work, your feet have to.

———

If you want something done—go. If you don't—send.

———

Always be aware of the consequences.

———

Always expect the worst, and when it comes, make the best of it.

———

Don't dig a foundation where you don't plan to build a house.

———

Don't take a single thing for granted—ever.

———

Never lower yourself to act like the opposition.

Mayann Armstrong

If they don't want to play with you, then you don't want to play with them.

———

It's not so important what happens to you in life as how you deal with what happens.

———

Try not to associate with anyone you can't learn something from.

———

Life is what you make it.

Constance Bicknell Auden

Birds and Bees,
Boys and Girls

If you bite your nails, it shows you're boy-crazy.

———

Go out with him—you don't know who you'll meet.

———

Don't let that boy spend too much money on you.

———

Treat all girls as if they were your sister.

———

For every Jack, there is a Jill.

Myra Edith Cutler Keaton

Where cobwebs grow,
there comes no beau.

———

All men are the same. They just have different faces so you can tell them apart.

———

You'd better marry a man who'll give you a personal maid.

———

No girl you marry is going to pick up after you.

———

If you stoop to marry, you'll never get up.

———

Don't make yourself too available.

———

Don't cheapen yourself.

———

Never advertise what you don't have for sale.

———

Petting is for animals.

———

No man chases a streetcar he's already caught.

Janet Woodrow Wilson

"Don't Play With Your Food!"

Stop pushing your food around on the plate.

_____

You eat what's put in front of you.

_____

Your eyes are bigger than your stomach.

_____

Never eat tuna fish at a drugstore.

_____

Eating ice will give you a stomach ache.

143

Frances Roche Shand-Kydd

Don't eat the last inch of a cucumber—it's poisonous.

———

Always pull off the strings on a banana—they give you a stomach ache.

———

Liverwurst is something you eat ten minutes before you die.

———

An orange is gold in the morning, silver at noon, and lead at night.

———

Eating celery is good for the nervous system.

———

As soon as you can count twelve bubbles, turn the pancakes.

———

Only take a little on the first helping.

———

Don't make a pig of yourself.

———

Always eat three square meals a day.

———

Always order from the middle of the menu.

Carol Joyce Anderson Ride

Don't eat in front of your friends unless you have enough to share.

———

Meat is tougher where there's none.

Janet Lee Bouvier Auchincloss

"Do You Want Me to Call the Doctor?"

You've only got one body, and you'd better take good care of it.

———

Don't smoke—it'll stunt your growth.

———

A cigarette has a fire on one end and a fool on the other.

———

If you wear galoshes inside, you'll get a headache.

———

Germs multiply on little hands.

149

Elzire Legros Dionne

Always take the cotton out of the pill bottle—it collects germs.

———

Don't crack your knuckles—you'll get arthritis.

———

Don't sit on the cold ground—you'll get galloping consumption.

———

Don't go outside with wet hair—you'll get pneumonia.

———

A little fresh air wouldn't kill you.

———

Remember, you can get sunburned on a cloudy day.

———

The important thing is to drink plenty of fluids.

Jana Semanska Navratilova

Practically Speaking

How you behave at home is how you'll behave outside the house.

_____

If you're bored, why don't you pick up your room?

_____

Time to change your clothes and put your apron on.

_____

Never leave the kitchen empty-handed.

_____

If you make a mess, you're going to have to clean it up.   153

Gloria Morgan Vanderbilt

If I let you get a dog [cat, bird, fish, hamster, etc.], I'll be the one who winds up feeding it.

———

Fish and company smell after three days.

———

Don't stand there with the refrigerator door open—everything will defrost.

———

Turn out the lights. We don't own stock in the electric company.

———

We don't *own* the Edison—we *owe* it.

———

Flowers should always look "happy" in a vase.

———

If you leave things behind at other people's houses, you'll never be invited back.

———

Never give a purse without putting money in it.

———

Always look down the chute a second time whenever you put a letter in the mailbox.

———

Make a reservation. You can always cancel it.

Emily Norcross Dickinson

The Tried
and True

How do you know you don't like it if you haven't tried it?

———

Don't throw out dirty water until you have clean.

———

It's always the weeds that grow the best.

———

What goes around comes around.

———

Sorry doesn't mend it.   157

Anna Rachel Berman Asimov

Manners maketh man.

———

One step at a time is all it takes to get there.

———

What's past hope is past grief.

———

There's a place for everything and everything in its place.

———

Things done by halves are never done right.

———

A quitter never wins and a winner never quits.

———

You're only as old as you feel.

———

Don't cut off your nose to spite your face.

———

Look it up—you'll remember it longer.

Evangelia Dimitriadis Calogeropoulos

Big Mom Is Watching You

You're not going out like *that*, are you?

———

Stop frowning—you'll be old before you're thirty.

———

Remember to smile—it's an improvement.

———

Don't you think people look at the back of your hair, too?

———

Your hair's not clean till it squeaks.

161

Fanny Schneider Mailer

Show me the backs of your hands.

———

Do your nails really taste *that* good?

———

X Y Z—Examine Your Zipper.

———

K Y L C—Keep Your Legs Crossed.

———

And this time make sure you use soap!

Kate Adams Keller

Mom Gets Folksy

Promises are like pie crusts—they're made to be broken.

———

If you're scared of the dark, remember the Ark.

———

I'll show you how the cow ate the cabbage.

———

Only the spoon that stirs the pot knows its troubles.

———

If wishes were pots and pans, there wouldn't be any tinners.

Flora Amelia Rivé Leonard

When you look at your feet, your feathers fall.

———

Still waters run deep, but the devil's at the bottom.

———

There *is* a devil, there is no doubt.
—But is he trying to get inside of us or out?

———

Cleft in the chin,
—Devil within.

———

The devil has many tools, and the lie is the handle that fits them all.

———

"It won't be long now," said the monkey with his tail cut off.

———

As you slide down the banister of life, don't get a splinter in your career.

———

If you burn your tail, you're going to have to sit on the blister.

———

Two wrongs don't make a right, but two Wrights made an airplane.

———

Don't spit up in the air—it'll fall on your nose.

Mary Walsh James

What's poured over the horse's back will meet under his belly.

———

Don't swallow the bull and leave the tail hanging out.

———

It'll never be noticed on a galloping horse.

Acknowledgments

I'd like to thank all the friends and friends of friends who helped: Patrick Ahern, Deborah Amos, Marian Babson, Jane Barlow, Reid Beddow, Betty Bloch, Ron Bloch, Ellen Boyers, Amanda Burden, Maurice Braddell, Taylor Branch, Joan Brandt, Sam Brown, Art Buchwald, Elisabeth Bumiller, Jonathan Carroll, Diane Cleaver, Mary Lee Coffey, Barbara Cohen, Richard Cohen, Janet Coleman, Jan Deeb, Alice Digilio, Michael Dirda, Mary Ann Donovan, Susan Dooley, Jan Drews, Nancy Dutton, Gayle Engel, Garrett Epps, Nick Eskidge, Kitty Ferguson, Pie Friendly, Harriett Gilbert, Lynn Goldberg, Bonnie Goldstein, Judy Green, Linda Greider, Christina Hammond, Rick Hertzberg, Barbara Howson, Mary Jarrett, Martha Jewett, Kathy Jones, Betsy Kane, Leslie Kantor, Stan Kantor, Steve Kelman, Meg King, Nina King, Stephen King, Michael Kinsley, Michaela Kurz, Myla Lerner, Gail Lynch, Mark Lynch, Christy Macy, Evan Marshall, Judith Martin, Kathy Matthews, Triny McClintock, Patricia McGerr, Marilyn Mitchell, Gene-Gabriel Moore, Nancy Pepper, Susan Percy, Claudine Peyre, Terry Pristin, Dermot Purgavie, Sally Quinn, Eden Rafshoon, Jerry Rafshoon, Eleanor Randolph, Coates Redmon, George Rider, Glenn Roberts, Paula Roberts, David Rubenstein, Wilfrid Sheed, Victoria Sloan, Amanda Smith, Caron Smith, Margaret Stannek, Alison Teal, John Teal, Susan Teal, Tom Teal, Val Teal, George W.S. Trow, Judith Van Ingen, Lydia Viscardi, Nicholas von Hoffman, Elsa Walsh, Jim Weisman, Steve Weisman, Celeste Wesson, Marjorie Williams, Doug Winter, Millicent Woods, Bob Woodward, Emily Yoffe.

Special thanks, too, go to: Gene Barnes, Sallie Bingham, 171

Victoria Haines, Michael Patrick Hearn, Margo Howard, Mona Joseph, Jim Lardner, Robert Phelps, Mildred Schwartz, Louis Sheaffer, Wendell Willkie II.

———

Again, I'd like to thank all the friends, friends of friends, mothers of friends, and friends who are mothers—not to mention the kind readers and radio and TV audiences—who shared "more momilies" with me: Elkan Abramowitz, Juliet Annan, Ronald Ball, Jack Bogat, Joe Brown, Karen Budirsky, Nancy Coffey, Barbara Cohen, Jack Cole, Robert (Chip) Cunningham, Judy-Lynn del Rey, Herb Denton, Connie Drummer, Berry Dyson, the Flynn family, Lynn Goldberg, Robert Goldstein, Liza Graham, Karen Gundersheimer, Russ Gould, Jana Harris, Barbara Howson, Susan Isaacs, Mary Jarrett, Leslie Kobylinski, Mrs. Paul C. Lyles, Robert Masello, Marilyn McCallum, Inez McClintock, John Meyers, Olivia Miles, Charlene Parker, Marcy Posner, Jody Powell, Bonnie Prudden, Eden Rafshoon, Laurie Rovtar, Lorraine Shanley, David Snyder, Susan Stamberg, Faith Stone, Jane Stubbs, Ednamae Storti, Margaret Ward, Sister Agnes Clare Warren, Liz Williams, Dan Yergin, Susan Zises.

Special thanks, too, go to: Stuart Applebaum, Robert Harrell, Edward Mendelson, Sylvia Morris, and Mark Ricci.

Key To Photographs